Contents

What is a settlement? 4

Towns and cities 8

Homes and businesses 12

Services 16

Getting around 20

Around the world 24

Changes 28

Checklist 30

Glossary 31

Index 32

Some words are shown in bold, **like this**. You can find out what they mean by looking in the glossary.

What is a settlement?

A settlement is a place where people live. Some settlements are home to many people. Others are very small.

4

This farmhouse in the countryside is a settlement all by itself.

Many settlements were built next to a river, where there is fresh water.

Some settlements are new. Others are hundreds of years old. In a settlement, people can work, play, and share **services**, such as hospitals and schools, with each other.

5

A small group of houses is called a hamlet. A slightly larger settlement is a village.

 This village is high up in the mountains.

Villagers' homes can be made of different things. Builders use materials that come from their local area. Here are some common building materials:

➠ wood

➠ stone

➠ brick

➠ dried mud.

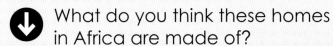 What do you think these homes in Africa are made of?

Towns and cities

Over hundreds of years some villages grow into much larger settlements. These are called towns. The biggest settlements are called cities.

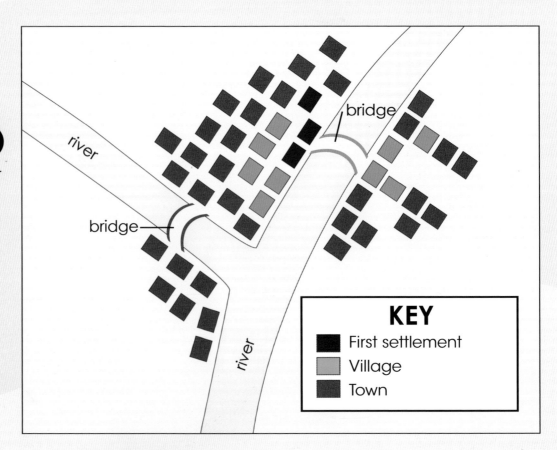

A tiny settlement can grow into a village, then into a town.

KEY

- First settlement
- Village
- Town

Q What do people do at a street market?

? **CLUE**

- Why do people bring money to a market?

People buy and sell things at a market.

Many old towns have a market square. This is where farmers used to bring their food to sell. People still have **market days** in towns. Today, most town and city people buy their food in supermarkets.

The world's biggest cities have millions of people.

skyscraper

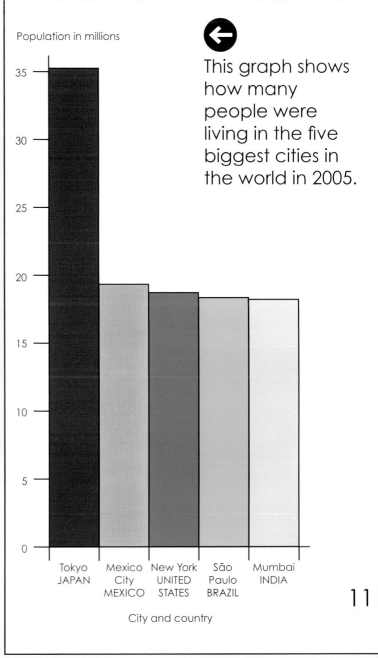

Population in millions

This graph shows how many people were living in the five biggest cities in the world in 2005.

City and country	Population

Tokyo JAPAN · Mexico City MEXICO · New York UNITED STATES · São Paulo BRAZIL · Mumbai INDIA

City and country

Tokyo is the capital of Japan. It is the world's largest city.

Homes and businesses

block of flats

house

Towns and cities are full of houses that people live in. Some people live in flats in large **tower blocks**.

Q Where are these people having their **picnic**?

? CLUES

- It is a large open space.
- It has lots of grass and trees.
- There are play areas.

13

They are having their **picnic** in a park.

14 Parks are open spaces where people can enjoy themselves. They are like large gardens. In towns and cities, people go to parks to get fresh air and relax. There are usually playgrounds where children can have fun.

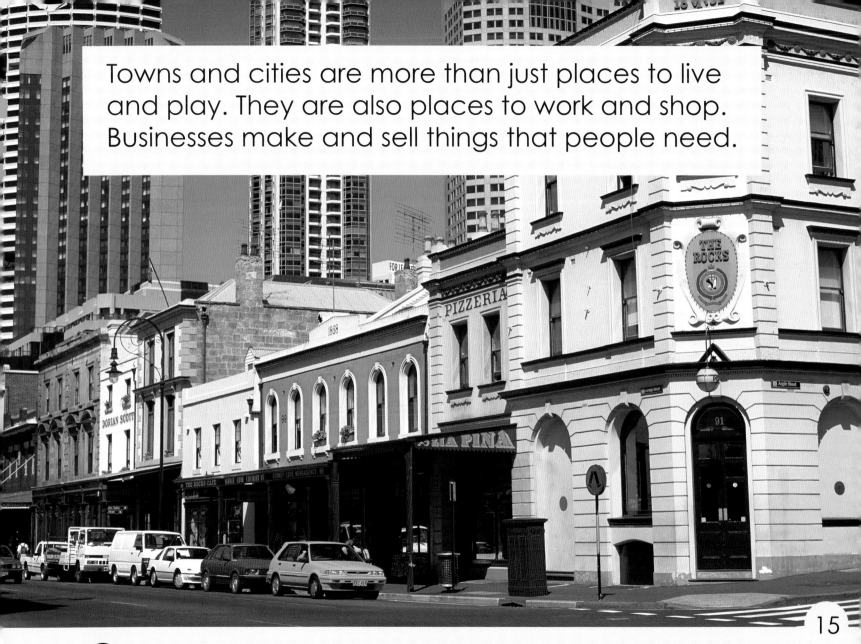

Towns and cities are more than just places to live and play. They are also places to work and shop. Businesses make and sell things that people need.

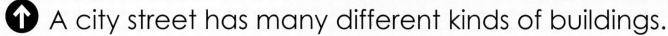

⬆ A city street has many different kinds of buildings.

Services

Villages, towns, and cities have schools, hospitals, and other **services**. The people who live there share these services.

All these services help people:
- fire stations
- hospitals
- libraries
- police stations
- post offices
- **refuse** collectors
- schools.

16

Q Where does this person work?

17

? **CLUES**

- She helps people if they are ill or injured.
- She helps people in an emergency.

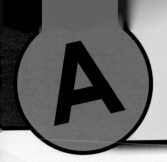

Local doctors have their own **surgery**, where people can go if they feel unwell. The doctor may send them to hospital, where they can have special treatment.

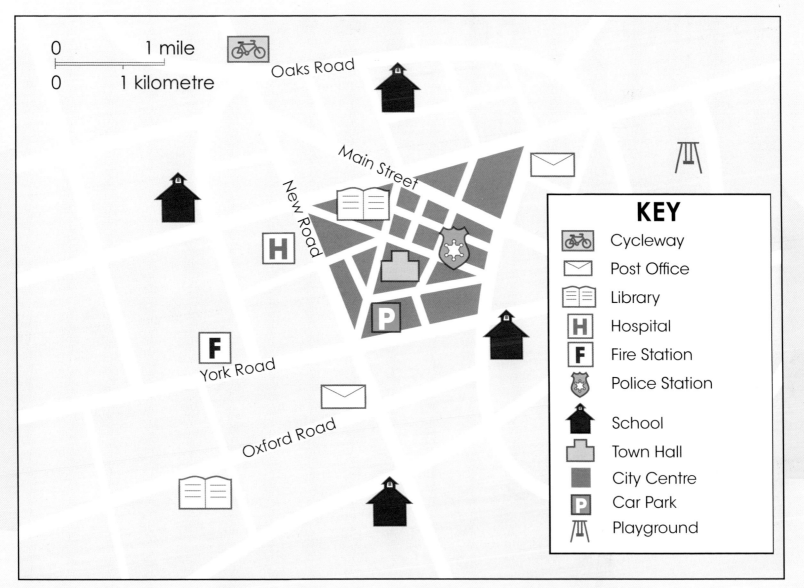

KEY

🚲	Cycleway
✉	Post Office
📖	Library
H	Hospital
F	Fire Station
🛡	Police Station
🏠	School
🏛	Town Hall
▨	City Centre
P	Car Park
⛓	Playground

Oaks Road

Main Street

New Road

York Road

Oxford Road

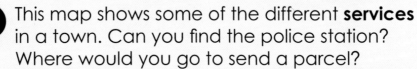

This map shows some of the different **services** in a town. Can you find the police station? Where would you go to send a parcel?

19

Getting around

Towns and cities have many roads and railways. They make it easy for people to get from one place to another. Roads and railways also link different places to each other.

This diagram shows the railway and bus routes in a town.

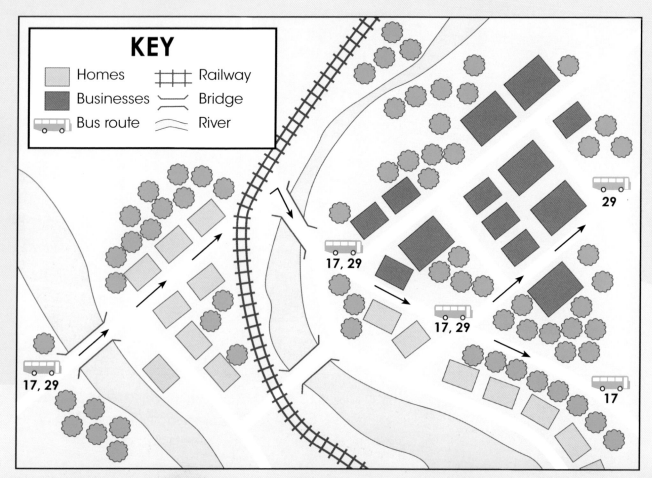

KEY

Homes
Businesses
Bus route
Railway
Bridge
River

17, 29

17, 29

17, 29

29

17

Q Which kind of transport does not need petrol?

? **CLUE**

- Human muscles do the work.

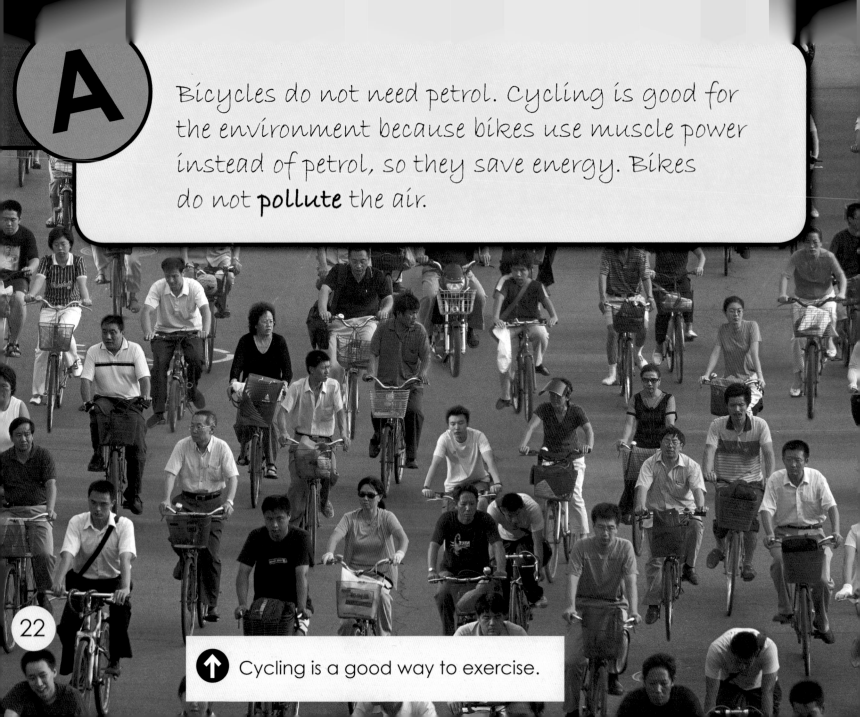

A Bicycles do not need petrol. Cycling is good for the environment because bikes use muscle power instead of petrol, so they save energy. Bikes do not **pollute** the air.

⬆ Cycling is a good way to exercise.

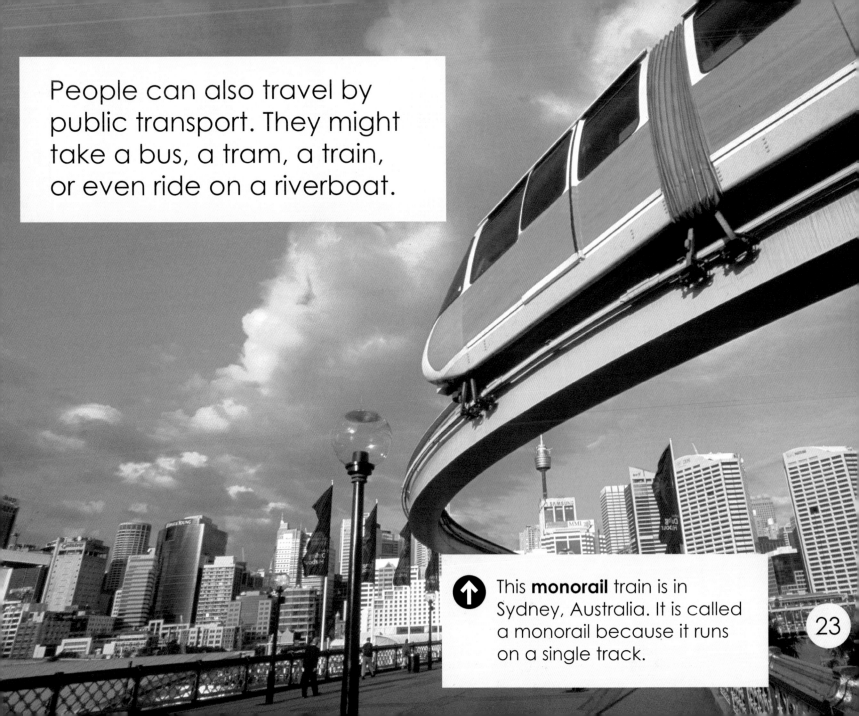

People can also travel by public transport. They might take a bus, a tram, a train, or even ride on a riverboat.

This **monorail** train is in Sydney, Australia. It is called a monorail because it runs on a single track.

23

Around the world

Settlements **vary** a lot in different parts of the world. A settlement in a hot place may be very different from one in a cold place. Settlements can also vary because people are either rich or poor.

↑ This **shanty town** is in a poor district of Ho Chi Minh City, in Vietnam.

Q Do you think this settlement is in Africa or North America?

? CLUES

- Much of Africa is hot.
- Parts of North America can be very cold in the winter.

25

A This is the town of Iqaluit, in Canada, part of North America.

26

People live different lives in different parts of the world. In northern Canada, many people travel about on **snowmobiles**.

snowmobile

Changes

Settlements change over time. Some small settlements grow into big towns or large cities.

 The city of Detroit, USA, grew into a city because of factories making cars.

People first lived in Paris, France thousands of years ago. At first it was a small settlement on the banks and islands of the River Seine. Today it is home to millions of people.

⬆ This island in Paris was the city's first settlement.

Checklist

A settlement is a place where people live.

Some settlements are very old. Others are new. Settlements change over time.

Hamlets and villages are small settlements. Some grow into larger towns and cities.

Cities are the largest settlements. A big city, such as London or New York, is home to millions of people.

Settlements **vary** in different parts of the world. This is sometimes because of differences in the temperature and the weather that places usually get. Also, people are richer in some places than others.

Glossary

market day day of the week when a market is usually held

monorail railway that runs on a single track

picnic meal that is eaten outdoors

pollute damage with harmful substances

refuse rubbish

services buses, trains, police, post offices, and other systems that provide people with what they need

shanty town settlement of poorly made shacks

snowmobile vehicle like a motorbike for travelling on snow

surgery doctor's office, where he or she sees and treats patients

tower block tall building of flats or offices

vary to be different or change

Index

building materials 7
businesses 15

cycling 23

farmhouses 4

hamlets 6, 30
homes 12
hospitals 5, 17, 18
hot and cold places 24,
    25–27, 30

markets 9, 10

parks 14
pollution 22

populations 11

rich and poor
settlements 24, 30
rivers 5, 29
roads and railways
    20–21, 23

services 5, 16–19
shanty towns 24

tower blocks 12
towns and cities 8–15,
    16, 20, 26, 28–29, 30
transport 20–23, 27

villages 6, 7, 8, 16, 30